GOD'S GUIDE

to the

END TIMES

The Revelation of Jesus Christ In Plain English

I dedicate this book to my sons, Curtis and Daniel.

To contact the author, email:
witback @ gmail.com

Contents

FIRST INFORMATIVE INTERLUDE

144,000 Faithful Jews Sealed on Earth, before the Seventh Seal

All the Repentant of the Five Unfaithful Churches Safe in Heaven, before the Seventh Seal

THINGS YET FUTURE, CONTINUED

The Seventh Seal: Seven Trumpets of Christ's Authority

The First Six Trumpets

THINGS PAST AND PRESENT

Christ's Representative Angel's Authority over the Unrepentant World

Christ's Message to the Unrepentant World

THINGS YET FUTURE, CONTINUED

Christ's Evaluation of all the Jews in Israel, before the Seven Vials

Christ's Worthiness Proclaimed by Two Faithful Jews on Earth, before the Seven Vials

The Seventh Trumpet: Seven Vials of God's Wrath

SECOND INFORMATIVE INTERLUDE

Summary of Satan's Campaign against the Israeli Nation

Summary of Satan's Campaign against Faithful Jews

Summary of the Antichrist's Campaign against Faithful Christians

Summary of the False Prophet's Deception of Unfaithful Jews

Summary of Christ's Catching-Up to Heaven of the Sealed Jews

Summary of the Final Call to the World for Repentance

INTRODUCTION TO CHRIST'S REVELATION

Revelation 1:1-8

This is the revelation of Jesus Christ, that God gave to Him, to show to His servants - Christians - the global trial and tribulation that must abruptly come upon the world. Christ sent this revelation and signified it with visual metaphors, via His representative angel, to His servant John. And John made the following written record of it, specifically what he saw, what he was told in general, and what message Christ gave him for Christians.

Endowed with God's favour are those who read and they who hear what John was told in general, and also comply with Christ's message to Christians. For the time is near in which this global trial and tribulation must abruptly come upon the world, and of all the people living on the eve of this trial and tribulation, only those who comply with Christ's message to Christians will be spared.

From John to the seven types of churches within Christendom, may graciousness at heart and reconciliation with God be supplied to you...
• from the eternal God,
• from the complete Spirit of God, which is the Spirit of the Lord, of Wisdom, Understanding, Counsel, Might, Knowledge, and Fear of the Lord,
• and from Jesus Christ, who being the eternal God incarnate is the faithful testament to God's will, and being the first resurrected from death to eternal life is the Saviour of humanity, and being the chief ruler of the kings of the earth is

the Lord of the world.

To Jesus Christ, who loved us, and washed us from our sins in his own blood shed upon the cross, and has made us worthy in God's sight to reign and serve in His kingdom, to him be glory and dominion for ever and ever. Amen.

Take special note, Jesus Christ will return to the Mount of Olives with majesty and strength, to restore God's kingdom upon this earth for a millennium, and all those who are gathered there for the battle of Armageddon, and all the Jews in Israel, will see Him return. And every ethnic group on the earth will wail because of Him as He executes the completion of God's wrath upon the entire unrepentant world. Even so, Amen.

I am Alpha and Omega, the beginning and the ending - the author of God's plan of salvation from creation through to eternity - says the Lord Jesus Christ, the eternal God, the Almighty.

Part One

CHRIST'S REVELATION
TO THE CHURCHES

Chapter One

THINGS PAST AND PRESENT

Revelation 1:9-20; 2:1-29; 3:1-22.

Christ's Authority over Christendom

John, a Christian brother and companion in localized tribulation, in the kingdom of God, and in endurance in the Christian faith, was detained on the island called Patmos for declaring the general truth from God, and Christ's message specifically to Christians.

At some time while there on Patmos, John was immersed in the Spirit of God concerning the day in which Christ will execute the completion of God's wrath upon the entire unrepentant world. Then he heard behind him the assertive voice of the Lord Jesus Christ, saying, I am the author of God's plan of salvation from creation through to eternity. What you see, write it in a book, and send it to the seven churches that are in Asia. These seven churches represent the seven types of churches within all Christendom.

John then turned to see who was talking to him. And having turned, he saw Christ standing in the midst of the seven types of churches within all Christendom, dressed as high priest, characterized as the express image of God, the instrument of God's vengeance, and the appointed agent of God's righteous judgment, speaking with the full authority of God, having complete authority over all the ministers of all Christendom, with His words depicted as the instrument of God's righteous judgment, and His face as the expression of God's righteousness.

Christ's authority over Christendom,
vividly illustrated. Rev 1:12-16.

And when he saw Christ, John fell at His feet as if he was dead. But Christ placed His authoritative hand on John, and told him not to be afraid, because He is the author of God's plan of salvation from creation through to eternity, who personally entered hell and then resurrected Himself from death, and therefore has complete control over entrance to hell and resurrection from death.

Christ then told John to write down the things that he had just seen i.e. Christ's authority over Christendom vividly illustrated, and the things that are yet present i.e. Christ's following message to Christians within the seven types of churches within all Christendom, and the things that will happen in the future i.e. after the Church Age.

Christ then gave an example of how to translate the visual metaphors within this Revelation, by Himself translating part of the very first one, which John had just seen. Christ explained that the seven stars which John had just seen in His right hand, are the ministers of the seven types of churches within all Christendom, and that the seven candlesticks are the seven types of churches, whose purpose is to bear enlightenment concerning God's will in a spiritually ignorant world.

Christ's Message to the Doctrinally Disloyal

See Chart, Image 1

To the doctrinally disloyal. Rev 2:1-7.

Christ then told John to write the following message to all those who are doctrinally disloyal within Christendom, typified by those faithful to Brethren teaching:

These things says the one who has complete authority over all the ministers of Christendom, and who walks in the midst of the seven types of churches within Christendom, and is therefore in the position to remove any type of church from God's household.

I, the Lord Jesus Christ, know all the Christian works that you have done, and your labour in the gospel, and your endurance in the Christian faith, and how you cannot bear self-centered religious leaders, and have tried them that falsely say they are ambassadors of the gospel, and found them to be liars, and have suffered false witness against you, and endured it because of your faith in Me, and have laboured in the gospel for My name's sake, and have not lost conviction under localized tribulation.

Nevertheless, I have something against you. You have forsaken your first love. You have forsaken My doctrine - the teaching that God's subjects must bear kindness and consideration [love] towards all people irrespective of persons.

Remember therefore from where you have fallen, from the Spirit of God's graciousness contained within My teaching. Then repent, and do the first Christian works i.e. comply with the essential doctrine of Christianity - that God's subjects must bear kindness and consideration towards all people irrespective of persons. For if you do not, then I will come upon you unexpectedly like a thief comes in the night, at the end of the global trial and tribulation to come. And I will then remove your type of church out of God's household, and appoint it a place in hell with the unbelievers, unless you repent beforehand.

Be encouraged to repent and do my works, by the fact that you hate the works of self-centered religious leaders, who falsely say they are ambassadors of the gospel, who I also hate.

Let whoever has a spiritual ear, hear the essence of My message to the seven types of churches within Christendom. To those who overcome their self-centeredness with God's indwelling Spirit of graciousness, to them will I give to eat of the tree of eternal physical life, that is in the midst of the paradise of God.

Christ's Message to the Doctrinally Valiant

See Chart, Image 2

To the doctrinally valiant. Rev 2:8-11.

Christ then told John to write the following message to all those who are doctrinally valiant within Christendom, typified by those fatefully faithful to Christ's teaching:

These things says the author of God's plan of salvation from creation through to eternity, who personally entered hell and then resurrected Himself from death, and therefore has complete control over entrance to hell and resurrection from death.

I, the Lord Jesus Christ, know all the Christian works that you have done, and the localized tribulation that you suffer, and the contriteness of your heart. But you are rich, in that you have reward in heaven. In contrast, I also know the blasphemy of those Jews who falsely claim to be true believers and thus contrite at heart.

Fear none of those things that you will suffer. Take special note, the devil will cast some of you into prison so that your faith in Me may be tried, and you will suffer localized tribulation because of your faith. Remain faithful to Me, by consistently complying with my commands until your physical death, and I will give you a crown of eternal life.

Let whoever has a spiritual ear, hear the essence of My message to the seven types of churches within Christendom. Those who overcome their self-centeredness with God's indwelling Spirit of graciousness, they will not suffer eternal spiritual death in the lake of fire.

Christ's Message to the Doctrinally Compromising

See Chart, Image 3

To the doctrinally compromising. Rev 2:12-17.

Christ then told John to write the following message to all those who are doctrinally compromising within Christendom, typified by those faithful to Presbyterian teaching:

These things says the one whose words are the instrument of God's righteous judgment.

I, the Lord Jesus Christ, know all the Christian works that you have done, and that you dwell where idolatry is dominant in society, and yet you continue to confess My name, and have not denied the Christian faith, even in the days when Christians were martyred for confessing their faith.

But I have a few things against you. You have in your type of church those who hold the doctrine of Balaam - the teaching that God's subjects are in an unconditional covenant relationship with God. You also have those who hold the doctrine of the Nicolaitans - the teaching that God's subjects are under the authority of religious leaders, which I hate.

Repent, or else I will come upon you unexpectedly like a thief comes in the night, at the end of the global trial and tribulation to come. And I will then fight with the righteous judgment of

My words, against those of you who live as though salvation is unconditional, and against those of you who reverence religious leaders, unless you repent beforehand.

Let whoever has a spiritual ear, hear the essence of My message to the seven types of churches within Christendom. To those who overcome their self-centeredness with God's indwelling Spirit of graciousness, to each of them will I give the hidden wisdom of God, absolution, and a new name of adoption into God's household.

Christ's Message to the Doctrinally Corrupt

See Chart, Image 4

To the doctrinally corrupt. Rev 2:18-29.

Christ then told John to write the following message to all those who are doctrinally corrupt within Christendom, typified by those faithful to Catholic teaching:

These things says the Son of God, who is the instrument of God's vengeance, and the appointed agent of God's righteous judgment.

I, the Lord Jesus Christ, know all the Christian works that you have done, and your kindness, and your charitableness, and your confidence of salvation, and your endurance in the Christian faith, and all the works that you are still doing, which are actually better than the works that you did at first.

Notwithstanding, I have a few things against you. You indulge that woman, the embodiment of the spirit of Babylon, who falsely claims that she has divine revelation. You allow this spirit to corrupt those under my authority concerning God's will, by allowing her to teach and seduce them to join divine revelation with false religious beliefs, and to eat things sacrificed to idols.

Take special note, I will cast this spirit of Babylon and those Christians who commit spiritual adultery with her, into the global trial and tribulation to come, unless they repent beforehand of their unfaithfulness to Me. I will then put them all to death. And all Christendom will thereby know that I am the one who searches the minds and hearts. And I will give to every one of you according to your works. To those of you who do your own will, I will give eternal damnation. To those of you who do God's will, I will give eternal life.

To the rest of you in this type of church who do not hold to this adulterous doctrine, and have not been seduced by this satanic spirit, I will put no other burden upon you other than that you hold fast to my doctrine until I return.

Let whoever has a spiritual ear, hear the essence of My message to the seven types of churches within Christendom. To those who overcome their self-centeredness with God's indwelling Spirit of graciousness, until the end, to them will I give the authority to rule with a rod of iron over the nations during the restored kingdom of God upon this earth for a millennium. And I will give to them the emblem of supreme overseer.

Christ's Message to the Doctrinally Negligent

See Chart, Image 5

To the doctrinally negligent. Rev 3:1-6.

Christ then told John to write the following message to all those who are doctrinally negligent within Christendom, typified by those faithful to Baptist teaching:

These things says the one who has the complete Spirit of God, which is the Spirit of the Lord, of Wisdom, Understanding, Counsel, Might, Knowledge, and Fear of the Lord. And who has complete authority over all the ministers of all seven types of churches within Christendom. And therefore has complete control over both the direct supply and the administering of true enlightenment.

I, the Lord Jesus Christ, know all the Christian works that you have done, which have given you the reputation of being spiritually alive or enlightened, when in fact you are spiritually dead or unenlightened.

Be doctrinally vigilant, and strengthen what elements of My doctrine that you still hold, which are ready to die. For I have not found your bearing of kindness and consideration to be towards all people irrespective of persons.

Remember from where you learned that you are to be kind and considerate towards all people i.e. from My doctrine. Then hold fast to My doctrine - the teaching that God's subjects <u>must</u> bear kindness and consideration [love] towards all people irrespective of persons. Repent, or else I will come upon you unexpectedly like a thief comes in the night, at the end of the global trial and tribulation to come. And you will not know when I will come upon you, because you will be full of ignorance or misunderstanding - darkness - concerning God's will.

That being said, there are a few people in this type of church who have not defiled their God given robe of righteousness by being self-centered. They will walk with me in undefiled righteousness. For they are worthy in that they, through mutual kindness and consideration, endeavour to maintain oneness with all who hold the essence of My doctrine, which is impartial kindness and consideration.

Let whoever has a spiritual ear, hear the essence of My message to the seven types of churches within Christendom. Those who overcome their self-centeredness with God's indwelling Spirit of graciousness, they will be clothed in righteousness that is not defiled by their self-centeredness. And I will not blot out their names from the book of eternal life. Indeed, I will confess their names before my Father, and before his holy angels.

Christ's Message to the Doctrinally Vigilant

See Chart, Image 6

To the doctrinally vigilant. Rev 3:7-13.

Christ then told John to write the following message to all those who are doctrinally vigilant within Christendom, typified by those dutifully faithful to Christ's teaching:

These things says the one who is undefiled, who is honest, and who has sovereign possession of the key to God's kingdom, and therefore complete control over entrance to God's temple therein.

I, the Lord Jesus Christ, know all the Christian works that you have done. Take special note, I have opened for you the door to God's temple, and no one can shut it. For you still have a little strength, and have kept my teaching, and have thereby not denied that I alone am the Saviour and the Lord.

Take special note, I will make those Jews who falsely claim to be true believers, come and worship at your feet, and know that I have loved you who overcome your self-centeredness with God's indwelling Spirit of graciousness.

Because you have kept My doctrine, which defines the works that must accompany endurance in the Christian faith, I will keep you from the global trial and tribulation that must abruptly come upon the world in order to try the faith of the five unfaithful types of churches still dwelling on earth.

Take special note, I will come upon unfaithful Christians like a thief comes in the night. Hold fast to My doctrine - the teaching that God's subjects must bear kindness and consideration towards all people irrespective of persons - and thereby ensure that you will receive your crown of righteousness.

Let whoever has a spiritual ear, hear the essence of My message to the seven types of churches within Christendom. Those who overcome their self-centeredness with God's indwelling Spirit of graciousness, I will make them permanent fixtures in God's temple, in the new Jerusalem. And I will write God's name upon them, and also the name of God's city - the new Jerusalem, and also my new name.

Christ's Message to the Doctrinally Apathetic

See Chart, Image 7

To the doctrinally apathetic. Rev 3:14-22.

Christ then told John to write the following message to all those who are doctrinally apathetic within Christendom, typified by those faithful to Pentecostal teaching:

These things says the supreme authority, the faithful and true testament to God's will, the eternal God incarnate.

I, the Lord Jesus Christ, know all the Christian works that you have done, and that you neither reject nor accept My doctrine. I wish that you would either reject or accept it.

So then because you are unenthusiastic about My doctrine, neither rejecting nor accepting the teaching that God's subjects <u>must</u> bear kindness and consideration - love - towards all people irrespective of persons, I will eject you out of God's household, to receive your share of hell with the unbelievers.

You say that you are spiritually rich, and increased with goods, and have need of nothing. You do not realize that you are unhappy because you are being chastened by God, and miserable because you are self-deceived, and spiritually poor because you have no treasure in heaven, and oblivious to the Truth, and not covered with the God given robe of righteousness.

Because of this, I counsel you to obtain from Me a valuable testament to God's will, so that you may have treasure in heaven, and a robe that is not defiled by your self-centeredness, so that you may be clothed in God's righteousness. I counsel you also to apply My doctrine to your perception - to live in accordance with it - so that you may comprehend through experience the genuine love of God which is beyond mere knowledge.

I sharply criticize and discipline all those I love. Therefore be zealous, and repent.

Take special note, I - the Word of God incarnate - stand at the door to people's understanding, and knock. If anyone hears me, and opens their heart to me, I - the faithful and true testament to God's will - will come into them, and will share God's will with them.

Let whoever has a spiritual ear, hear the essence of My message to the seven types of churches within Christendom. To those who overcome their self-centeredness with God's indwelling Spirit of graciousness, even as I overcame self-centeredness, to them will I grant share of my power, riches, wisdom, strength, honour, glory and blessing.

Chapter Two

THINGS YET FUTURE

Revelation 4:1-11; 5:1-14; 6:1-17.

Christ's Evaluation of all Christians on Earth, before the Seven Seals

See Chart, Image 8

After Christ's message to the seven types of churches within Christendom - take special note - John then looked and saw a door open in heaven, a door to God's heavenly temple. And John heard the assertive voice of the Lord Jesus Christ talking to him from out of heaven, saying, Come up here, and I will show you things that must happen in the future i.e. after the Church Age.

John was then immediately caught-up in the Spirit of God to the temple in heaven. Take special note, John saw within the heavenly temple a throne, and sitting on it a representation of the eternal God and His sovereignty, and around it a rainbow signifying the reconciliation of humans to God at this throne.

And around the front of this throne of reconciliation, John saw twenty four seats, and sitting on them, twenty four elders of the Church, who collectively represent the body of faithful Christians miraculously caught-up to the heavenly temple at the end of the Church Age. John saw that they will be clothed in their undefiled God given robes of righteousness. And they will be wearing crowns of glory. These twenty four elders of the Church will be made up of one elder from each of the caught-up Church's twenty-four divisions, who in rotation collectively represent the whole Church after the pattern of the

Levitical priesthood.

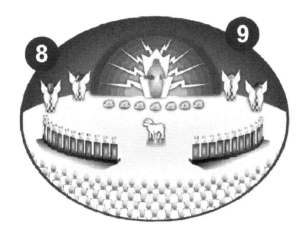

Those evaluated during their life to be faithful Christians,
will be present at the throne of reconciliation
in heaven. Rev 4:1-11.

From the throne itself comes lightning and thunder and voices. And burning in front of it are seven lamps of fire, which represent the complete Spirit of God - the Spirit of the Lord, of Wisdom, Understanding, Counsel, Might, Knowledge, and Fear of the Lord.

In front of the throne is a sea of crystal-like glass, signifying purity: holiness. And around the throne are four beasts, each covered front and back with many eyes, by which the Lord Jesus Christ sees every deed done by every person throughout the entire world.

Those faithful Christians evaluated during their life as producing a testament honourable to God will at this throne receive a great reward, whereas those faithful Christians evaluated as producing a testament dishonourable to God will at this throne receive no reward. Nonetheless all faithful Christians will be present at this throne before the outpouring of God's wrath upon the world at the end of the global trial and tribulation to come.

The first of these beasts around the throne is like a lion, signifying rule or authority, from minor regulations to God's sovereign rule. For this is its specific area of observation. The second beast is like a calf, signifying sacrifice or slaughter, from minor slander to genocide. For this is its specific area of observation. The third beast has a face like a man, signifying domination, from minor bullying to dictatorship. For this is its specific area of observation. The fourth beast is like a flying eagle, signifying deliverance, from minor intercessions to divine deliverance. For this is its specific area of observation.

All four beasts have six wings, and are covered within with many eyes, by which the Lord Jesus Christ swiftly sees every desire within every person's heart throughout the entire world. These beasts never cease saying, Holy, Holy, Holy, Lord God Almighty, the eternal God. For only those Christians evaluated during their life as being gracious at heart - holy - will be present at the throne of reconciliation to God.

And when these beasts give glory, honour and thanks to the eternal God sitting on the throne of reconciliation, the twenty four elders of the Church will fall down before Him, and worship Him, and cast their crowns of glory before the throne - thereby gesturing the caught-up Church's comparative unworthiness of glory. And they will say, You are worthy, O Lord, to receive glory and honour and power. For you have created all things, and you created them all for your pleasure.

Christ's Worthiness Proclaimed by the two Faithful Churches in Heaven, before the Seven Seals

See Chart, Image 9

John then saw a scroll in the authoritative hand of the eternal God, a scroll with writing on both the inside and the outside, and sealed with seven seals. And he saw that an angel with authority will proclaim, Who is worthy to open the scroll - to undo its seals, and thereby unleash God's seven year plan of global trial and tribulation upon the unrepentant self-centered world? But no human in heaven, on earth, or in hell, will be worthy to open the scroll, or even to look upon it.

John then wept much, because no human will be found worthy of authority over the world, not even of contemplating it.

But one of the twenty four elders of the Church then told John not to weep, and to take special note, that the Lion of the tribe of Judah, the descendant of king David, has on the cross prevailed over self-centeredness - over evil - and is therefore worthy to undo the scroll's seven seals, and thereby unleash God's plan of global trial and tribulation upon the unrepentant self-centered world.

And John took special note, and saw that Christ will then stand in front of the throne, and in the midst of the four beasts and the twenty four elders of the Church, depicted as the Saviour of humanity, having complete authority over the world, and having the complete Spirit of God - the Spirit of the Lord, of Wisdom, Understanding, Counsel, Might, Knowledge, and Fear of the Lord - which is sent throughout all the earth.

And Christ, the eternal God incarnate, will approach the throne of reconciliation, and will take the sealed scroll out of the authoritative hand of the representation of the eternal God and His sovereignty.

And the four beasts and the twenty four elders of the Church will fall down in front of Christ. The elders of the Church will each have harps, and golden vials full of the prayers of the Church - prayers for God's righteous will to be done on earth as it is in heaven.

And the Church - the body of faithful Christians miraculously caught-up to the heavenly temple at the end of the Church Age - will then sing a new song there in the heavenly temple, saying, You are worthy to take the scroll, and to open its seals. For you were crucified to pay for humanity's self-centeredness, and you have redeemed us to God by your blood, out of every ethnic group, language, people and nation. And you have made us kings and priests in God's sight, so that we will reign on the earth - in the kingdom of God restored on earth for a millennium following the global trial and tribulation to come.

John then again took special note, and heard that millions of holy angels around the throne, and around the beasts and the elders of the Church, will say with a loud voice, Worthy is Christ, the Lamb that was slain, to receive power, riches, wisdom, strength, honour, glory and blessing.

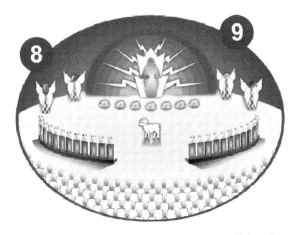

Christ's worthiness to open the seals, will be proclaimed by the two faithful churches in heaven. Rev 5:1-14.

And every angel stationed in heaven, on the earth, in hell, and in the sea of redemption, will collectively say, Blessing, honour, glory, and power, be to the representation of the eternal God, and to the eternal God incarnate, for ever and ever.

And the four beasts will say, Amen. And the twenty four elders of the Church will fall down and worship him that lives for ever and ever - the Lord Jesus Christ, the eternal God, the Almighty.

The First Seal: Peaceful Conquest

See Chart, Image 10

With an authoritative roar, the lion-like beast then told John to come and see what will happen when Christ opens the first seal of the scroll. For the opening of this first seal concerns this beast's specific area of observation: rule or authority.

A religious leader will confirm a peace treaty between the Israeli and Muslim nations. Rev 6:1-2.

Take special note, the spirit of conquest will be sent from heaven into the world. And riding this spirit of conquest will be a religious leader, who will bring temporary peace to the entire world. He will be given the right to rule. And he will be intent on conquering the world. This rider will be the Antichrist. Under this first seal, he will be hailed as the Savior of the world for confirming a seven year peace treaty between the Israeli and Islamic nations. Later under the fourth seal, he will set himself up in the rebuilt Jewish temple as god.

Christ will send this spirit of conquest upon the world in order to try the five unfaithful churches left on earth, with the intent of saving all those unfaithful Christians who, in response to this trial, repent and become faithful to Him.

The Second Seal: Outbreak of War

See Chart, Image 11

The calf-like beast then told John to come and see what will happen when Christ opens the second seal of the scroll. For the opening of this second seal concerns this beast's specific area of observation: sacrifice or slaughter.

A military leader will cause war. Rev 6:3-4.

The spirit of war will be sent from heaven into the world. And riding this spirit of war will be a military leader, who will end the temporary world peace brought about by the Antichrist, but not the seven year peace treaty between the Israeli and Islamic nations. He will make the inhabitants of the world go to war against one another, except for the Israeli and Islamic nations. And he will be given a mighty instrument of war by which to slaughter many.

Christ will send this spirit of war upon the world in order to try the five unfaithful churches left on earth, with the intent of saving all those unfaithful Christians who, in response to this trial, repent and become faithful to Him.

The Third Seal: Global Food Rationing

See Chart, Image 12

The man-like beast then told John to come and see what will happen when Christ opens the third seal of the scroll. For the opening of this third seal concerns this beast's specific area of observation: domination.

An executive will regulate global food rationing. Rev 6:5-6.

John then took special note, and saw that the spirit of famine will be sent from heaven into the world. And riding this spirit of famine will be an executive of an organization such as the Food and Agriculture Organization. He will establish food rationing throughout the entire world due to the famine. A ration of wheat from which bread is made will cost a day's wage. Three rations of barley by which livestock is fed will cost a day's wage. But vegetable oil and wine will not be affected.

Christ will send this spirit of famine upon the world in order to try the five unfaithful churches left on earth, with the intent of saving all those unfaithful Christians who, in response to this trial, repent and become faithful to Him.

The Fourth Seal: Death for the Repentant of the Five Unfaithful Churches

See Chart, Image 13

The eagle-like beast then told John to come and see what will happen when Christ opens the fourth seal of the scroll. For the opening of this fourth seal concerns this beast's specific area of observation: deliverance.

Satan will kill those who refuse to worship the Antichrist. Rev 6:7-8.

Take special note, the spirit of death will be sent from heaven into the world. And riding this spirit will be Satan. And following him will be his horde of demons. And they will be given authority for three and a half years over the entire world, to kill all those Christians on earth who refuse to worship the Antichrist, over a billion in total. They will kill with the sword those of them who are captured, and with hunger, death, and wild animals, those of them who manage to flee.

The Antichrist will be possessed by Satan under this fourth seal, and will then set himself up in the rebuilt Jewish temple as god. Also under this fourth seal, God will send strong delusion upon the unrepentant so that they will believe the

Antichrist. 2 Thess 2:8-12.

Christ will send this spirit of death upon the world in order to deliver to heaven all those of the five unfaithful churches who, in response to the preceding three trials and this tribulation, repent and become faithful to Him.

The Fifth Seal: The Repentant Vindicated in Heaven

See Chart, Image 14

John then saw what will happen when Christ opens the fifth seal of the scroll. The souls of all those killed under the fourth seal for not worshipping the Antichrist will then appear under the altar in the heavenly temple. These souls are those of the five unfaithful churches who, in response to the preceding trials and tribulation, repent and become faithful to Christ.

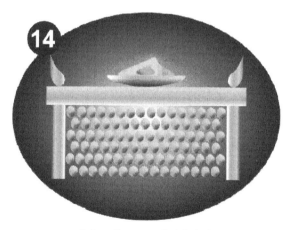

The repentant of the five unfaithful churches will be vindicated in heaven. Rev 6:9-11.

These souls will rightfully cry out from under the altar of martyred believers, asking the Lord Jesus how long it will be before He vindicates them by judging and avenging their blood on the unrepentant world who killed them.

They will all initially be vindicated by receiving their God given robes of righteousness. But they will have to wait until the remaining repentant of the five unfaithful churches have all been killed as they were, before being fully vindicated.

The Sixth Seal: The Unrepentant Roused on Earth

See Chart, Image 15

John then saw what will happen when Christ opens the sixth seal of the scroll. There will be a great upheaval in the world. The gospel of Jesus Christ, which defines righteousness, will cause great sorrow in the hearts of the unrepentant world because they refused to accept it. The law of Moses, which defines unrighteousness, will became unpalatable to the unrepentant world because they are condemned by it. And the divinely inspired prophesies concerning the outpouring of God's wrath upon the unrepentant world, will hit home.

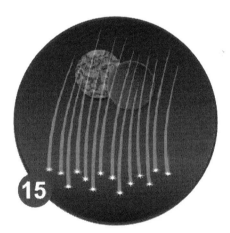

The gospel will cause mourning. The Law will become unpalatable. All prophecy will hit home. Rev 6:12-17.

For God will remove the strong delusion that He sent upon the unrepentant, so that they can understand the testimony of His two witnesses in Jerusalem, and thereby have a final opportunity to repent. And every dominant and subordinate kingdom will be awakened from their false sense of peace and safety, due to the testimony of God's two witnesses.

And the unrepentant of every class of people throughout the entire world will hide themselves in places of refuge, and in the defences of the most dominant kingdoms. And they will beg the most dominant kingdoms to use their defences to strike and bury them, in an attempt to hide from the righteous judgment of the eternal God, and from the wrath of Christ, the eternal God incarnate, who died on the cross to save them. And they will profess that the great day of Christ's wrath has come, and that no one will be able to withstand it. Yet they will not repent.

Continued on age 38, at Revelation 8:1.

Chapter Three

FIRST INFORMATIVE INTERLUDE

Revelation 7:1-17.

144,000 Faithful Jews Sealed on Earth, before the Seventh Seal

See Chart, Image 16

John then saw that four angels will then stand at the four corners of the earth, and will stop the four winds of the earth from blowing.

And another angel will then ascend from the east, having the seal of the true living God. This angel will command the four angels stopping the winds to not harm the earth, sea, or trees, until they have placed a seal on the foreheads of 144,000 of the Messianic Jews.

144,000 Messianic Jews will be sealed on earth. Rev 7:1-8.

Twelve thousand descendants of each of the twelve tribes of

Israel will then be sealed out of the Messianic Jews. Twelve thousand of the tribe of Judah, of the tribe of Reuben, of the tribe of Gad, of the tribe of Aser, of the tribe of Nephthalim, of the tribe of Manasses, of the tribe of Simeon, of the tribe of Levi, of the tribe of Issachar, of the tribe of Zabulon, of the tribe of Joseph, and of the tribe of Benjamin.

All the Repentant of the Five Unfaithful Churches Safe in Heaven, before the Seventh Seal

See Chart, Image 17

Then John saw that a great multitude of people, that no man could count, from all nations, kindreds, people, and tongues, will then stand before the throne of reconciliation in the heavenly temple, and before the Lord Jesus Christ, the agent of humanity's reconciliation to God. These people will all be clothed with undefiled God given robes of righteousness, and will all have palm branches in their hands, symbolizing their triumph over the Antichrist. And they will cry out that salvation is from God in heaven, and from the Lord Jesus Christ: God incarnate.

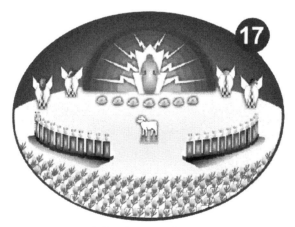

All the repentant of the five unfaithful churches will be in heaven before the day of God's wrath. Rev 7:9-17.

And all the holy angels will stand in the heavenly temple around the throne of reconciliation, and around the twenty four elders of the Church, and the four beasts. And they will fall before the throne on their faces, and worship God, Saying, Amen: Blessing, glory, wisdom, thanksgiving, honour, power, and might, be unto our God for ever and ever. Amen.

Then one of the twenty four elders of the Church asked John who these people in undefiled robes are, and where they come from. But John did not know. So the elder told him that they are the people who will come out of the great tribulation through martyrdom, having repented and become faithful to Christ and thereby washed their defiled robes of righteousness in Christ's blood and made them pure again. They will therefore be present before the holy throne of reconciliation in the heavenly temple, and will serve God day and night in his temple. And God will dwell among them. These are all those of the five unfaithful types of churches who repent and become faithful to Christ during the global trial and tribulation to come.

They will never again hunger for knowledge, or ever again thirst for understanding, or ever again endure God's righteous judgment upon them, or any fiery trial of their faith. For the Lord Jesus Christ will satisfy their hunger for knowledge of God, and will lead them unto living fountains of spiritual understanding. And God will wipe away all tears from their eyes, which they will have shed due to their suffering His righteous judgment and the trial of their faith.

Chapter Four

THINGS YET FUTURE, CONTINUED

Revelation 8:1-13; 9:1-21.

The Seventh Seal: Seven Trumpets of Christ's Authority

John then saw what will happen when Christ opens the seventh seal of the scroll. There will be solemn silence in heaven for about half an hour. Then seven angels will stand before God and His throne. And they will be given seven trumpets - instruments for asserting the Lord Jesus Christ's complete authority over His creation.

And another angel will come and stand at the altar of martyred believers before the throne. He will have a golden censer. And he will be given much incense to burn in the censer. This incense will be the prayers of all those martyred during the global trial and tribulation to come - their prayers for God to avenge their blood upon the unrepentant world, who killed them. And the angel will offer the prayers of the martyred upon the golden alter before the throne, along with the accumulated prayers of all faithful believers - their prayers for God to fulfil His will on earth as it is in heaven.

And the smoke of the incense and the prayers of all faithful believers will rise up before God. Then the angel will take the censer containing the prayers for vengeance and righteousness, and will fill it with fire from the altar of martyred believers. Then he will cast it into the earth. And out of the throne of reconciliation will come voices, thunderings, lightnings, and a great upheaval.

And the seven angels with the seven trumpets will then prepare to sound - to assert the Lord Jesus Christ's complete authority over His creation.

The First Six Trumpets

See Chart, Images 18-23

The first six trumpets. Rev 8:7-13; 9:1-21.

The first angel will then sound his trumpet, and one of the four angels stopping the winds of the earth will cast hail and fire mingled with blood upon the earth. This will cause a third of all trees and green grass to be burned up.

The second angel will then sound his trumpet, and another of the four angels stopping the winds of the earth will cast a great burning mountain into the sea. This will cause a third of the sea to become blood, a third of all sea creatures to die, and a third of all ships to be destroyed.

The third angel will then sound his trumpet, and another of the four angels stopping the winds of the earth will cause a great star, burning like a lamp, to fall from heaven upon a third of all the rivers and natural water fountains. This will make a third of all drinking water acidic, and cause the death of many people.

The fourth angel will then sound his trumpet, and another of the four angels stopping the winds of the earth will make the sun, moon and stars, go dark for a third of each of the following days and nights. This will cause great panic in the world.

And another angel will then fly across the sky, declaring three Woes to the inhabitants of the earth because of the three trumpets yet to be sounded. For the three remaining trumpets are specifically directed at people.

THE FIRST WOE

The fifth angel will then sound his trumpet, and a fallen angel will be given the key to the bottomless pit. This demon will then open the bottomless pit, releasing a smoke that will cause the sun and air to go dark.

Demonic beings will then come out of the smoke, into the world. These beings will be given the ability to sting people, like scorpions.

And the Lord Jesus Christ will command them not to hurt the 144,000 sealed of the Messianic Jews, but to hurt only those people who do not have the seal of God in their foreheads, including all non-Messianic Jews. Joel 2:4-11.

These demons will not have the ability to kill, but rather their sting will torment people for five months, like the torment of a scorpion sting. The people stung by these demons will want to die, but they will not be able to.

These demons will be the shape of horses reared up on hind legs prepared for battle. They will have golden crowns on their heads, symbolizing their imparted authority. And they will have human-like faces, symbolizing their dominance over humanity.

They will have long hair, symbolizing God's glory, and teeth like lions, symbolising Christ's justice. They will have breastplates like iron, symbolizing strength, and wings that sound like many horses and chariots running to battle. And they will be led by another demon from the bottomless pit. His name in Hebrew is Abaddon, but in Greek it is Apollyon.

This is the completion of the first woe. Take special note there are two more woes to follow immediately after each other.

THE SECOND WOE

The sixth angel will then sound his trumpet, and the Lord Jesus Christ's voice will be heard from the four horns of the golden altar of martyred believers in the heavenly temple, commanding the release of four fallen angels that are bound in the great Euphrates River. And these four angels will then be loosed. They have been reserved for this exact time, to kill a third of the earth's population - specifically those who are still worshipping idols.

These four fallen angels will have a two hundred million strong demonic cavalry under their command. And John saw that the riders of this demonic cavalry will have breastplates of fire and brimstone. And the horses will have heads of lions, which symbolize Christ's control of them. These demons will destroy by the spewing of fire, smoke and brimstone, out of their horses' mouths, which represents God's righteous judgment. And they will kill by the bite of the snake-like heads on their horses' tails, which represents the consequence of sin.

Despite this supernatural killing of approximately two billion idol worshippers, the rest of the world will not repent of their worshipping idols - their worshipping of things made of gold, silver, brass, stone, and wood, which cannot see, or hear, or walk. Nor will they repent of their part in the martyrdom of faithful believers, nor of their perceived supernatural practices, nor of their association with false religions, nor of their robbing God of glory.

Continued on page 48, at Revelation 11:1.

Part Two

CHRIST'S REVELATION
TO THE WORLD

Chapter One

THINGS PAST AND PRESENT

Revelation 10:1-11.

Christ's Representative Angel's Authority over the Unrepentant World

John then saw a mighty angel - the Lord Jesus Christ's angelic representative - coming down from heaven, clothed with Christ's majesty and strength. This angel bore Christ's message to the unrepentant world concerning humanity's reconciliation to God, God's righteousness, and Christ's following righteous judgment upon the unrepentant. For Christ does not speak directly to the unrepentant world.

Christ's representative angel's authority over the unrepentant world, vividly illustrated. Rev 10:1-11.

This angel had a little book open in his hand. And he set his right foot on the sea, signifying God's judgment upon the Gentile, or non-Jewish, nations. And he set his left foot on the earth, signifying God's judgment on the Israeli, or Jewish, nation. He then cried out with an authoritative voice, like a roaring lion, in expression of the Lord Jesus Christ's authority. And when he cried out, seven thunders spoke the complete authority of God.

John began to write down what the seven thunders said, but then stopped because he heard the assertive voice of the Lord Jesus Christ telling him not to write it down. For what the seven thunders said was not Christ's message, but rather a confirmation to John that the message has the complete authority of God.

Christ's Message to the Unrepentant World

The Lord Jesus Christ's mighty representative angel then lifted up his hand to heaven, and swore by the eternal God who created all things, that the time in which humanity may repent and be reconciled to God will end when the seventh trumpet sounds. For when the seventh trumpet sounds, God's work of reconciling both non-Jew and Jew to Himself in one body - the Church - will be complete.

John then heard the assertive voice of the Lord Jesus Christ speak to him again, telling him to go and take the little book from the mighty angel standing upon both the Israeli and Gentile nations.

So John went to the mighty angel and asked for the little book, which symbolizes Christ's message to the unrepentant world. And the angel told John to take it, and ingest it, and that it would make his belly bitter while tasting sweet in his mouth.

John then took the little book out of the angel's hand, and ingested it. And it tasted sweet in his mouth, but it then made his belly bitter. For Christ's message contains the sweet truth of reconciliation to God, and also the upsetting truth of the following judgment upon those not reconciled to God, both Gentile and Jew alike.

Christ's mighty representative angel then told John that he must prophesy again. That he must prophesy the following of this Revelation - symbolized by the little book - to the entire unrepentant world concerning God's coming judgment upon them.

All the Revelation preceding John's receipt of the little book is Christ's revelation directly to His servants - Christians - to show them the global trial and tribulation that must come upon the world. All the Revelation following John's receipt of the little book is Christ's revelation indirectly to the unrepentant world - both Gentle and Jew - to show them the global judgment that must come upon the world, and also the ultimate destiny of Satan and all humanity. For God being gracious gives everyone the opportunity to repent.

Chapter Two

THINGS YET FUTURE, CONTINUED

Revelation 11:1-19.

Christ's Evaluation of all the Jews in Israel, before the Seven Vials

See Chart, Image 24

John was then given a spiritual measuring rod, and told by the Lord's mighty representative angel to go and measure the rebuilt Jewish temple of God in Jerusalem, its altar, and the Jews who will worship therein, in order to evaluate how honourable a testament they are to God.

Jews in Israel will be evaluated after the church age. Rev 11:1-2.

But John was told not to measure the outer court of the temple, because it will be given to Gentiles - non-Jews - during this time of evaluation. For under the peace treaty confirmed by the Antichrist between the Israeli and Islamic nations, the Jewish temple mount will be shared by both Gentiles and Jews during the first half of the global trial and tribulation to come.

Christ's Worthiness Proclaimed by Two Faithful Jews on Earth, before the Seven Vials

See Chart, Image 25

The Lord's mighty representative angel then told John that Christ will then empower two witnesses for forty-two Jewish or 30 day months, to prophesy concerning His worthiness to judge the unrepentant world. These two witnesses will prophesy in Jerusalem for the entire second half of the global trial and tribulation to come, clothed in sackcloth, which symbolizes the Jewish people's need to repent.

These two witnesses will stand as preachers of divine reconciliation, and as living testaments to the worthiness of the God of heaven - Christ - in defiance of the god of the earth: Satan. And anyone who attempts to silence them will be killed by fire from their mouths.

Christ's worthiness will be proclaimed by two faithful Jews on earth. Rev 11:3:13.

The Lord's mighty representative angel will also empower Christ's two witnesses to stop the rain, turn rivers to blood, and bring plagues upon people - just like Elijah and Moses did. But as soon as the two witnesses have finished their three and a half year testimony concerning Christ's worthiness, the demon king Apollyon in possession of the Antichrist will immediately be allowed to attack and kill them.

Their dead bodies will then lie in the street of the great city Jerusalem, which spiritually is called ungodly and oppressive, where also our Lord Jesus Christ was crucified. And the world will watch their dead bodies lying on the ground for three and a half days, and will not allow them to be put in graves.

And Jews throughout the entire world will rejoice over their death, and make merry, and will send gifts to one another, because the two witnesses will have tormented them for the past three and a half years.

But after three and a half days, the spirit of life from God will enter into the two witnesses, and they will stand upon their feet. And great fear will fall upon all those who see it. Then, upon hearing the assertive voice of the Lord Jesus Christ from heaven saying to them, Come up here, the two witnesses will ascend up to heaven in a cloud. And their enemies will see them ascending.

There will then be a great earthquake that will cause a tenth of Jerusalem to collapse, and will kill seven thousand Jews. And the remaining Jews will be afraid, and will give glory to the God of heaven.

The Seventh Trumpet: Seven Vials of God's Wrath

Two woes have been completed, and - take special note - the third woe follows immediately after the second.

THE THIRD WOE

The seventh angel will then sound his trumpet, which constitutes the seven vials of God's wrath. And following the outpouring of these seven vials of God's wrath, there will be great voices in heaven, saying, The kingdoms of the world have now become the kingdoms of God in heaven and of Christ: God incarnate. And Christ will now reign for ever and ever over all earthly kingdoms, beginning on this present earth for a millennium, and continuing on the new earth to come for all eternity.

Then the twenty four elders of the caught up to heaven Church, sitting before God in the heavenly temple, will fall on their faces, and worship God, giving Him thanks for asserting His complete authority over the unrepentant world, and for the outpouring of His wrath upon the unrepentant world, and for the rewards awaiting the prophets and all who have repented and overcome worldliness, and also for the destruction of the unrepentant world's armies at the battle of Armageddon.

Then the temple of testimony will open in heaven, revealing the heavenly ark of God's testament containing God's law, which convicts people of sin and therefore condemns the unrepentant world to death. And out of the temple and the throne of reconciliation will come voices, thunders, and lightnings. Then a great earthquake will destroy all the kingdoms of the world. And great hail will fall upon the entire unrepentant world.

Continued on page 66, at Revelation 15:1.

Chapter Three

SECOND INFORMATIVE INTERLUDE

Revelation 12:1-17; 13:1-18; 14:1-20.

Summary of Satan's Campaign against the Israeli Nation

See Chart, Images 26-29

John then saw a great wonder in the sky, God's wife - the nation of Israel - clothed with God's righteousness, with the Mosaic Law as the foundation upon which she stands, and the twelve tribes of Israel as her crowning glory. And he saw her cry out in labour, in pain about to give birth to the Lord Jesus Christ.

The Israeli nation about to give birth to Christ. Rev 12:1-2.

And another wonder appeared in the sky - take special note - John saw Satan, the devil, having the seven most dominant consecutive kingdoms and empires of man under his complete control, and also the ten most prominent countries into which the last of these empires will divide.

Satan reigning via the seven most dominant kingdoms of man, waiting to devour Christ at His birth. Rev 12:3-4.

The seven most dominant consecutive kingdoms and empires of man are: Sumer, Egypt, Assyria, Babylon, Persia, Greece, and Rome. And the ten most prominent countries into which the last of these empires will divide are most likely: Britain, France, Germany, Italy, Spain, Greece, Turkey, Egypt, Iraq, and Iran.

And John saw that Satan caused a third of the heavenly angels to follow him, and also that he used his complete control over the Roman empire to stand before the nation of Israel when she was about to give birth to Christ, in an attempt to devour Him as soon as he was born, in approximately 4 BC.

And John saw that the nation of Israel gave birth to the Lord Jesus Christ, that Christ will rule all the nations with a rod of iron for a millennium, and that He was caught up to God and his throne of reconciliation in heaven in approximately 29 AD, despite Satan's efforts to devour Him.

Christ was caught-up to heaven following His resurrection. Rev 12:5.

And John saw that those of the nation of Israel who are still faithful to Jehovah will flee from Jerusalem into the wilderness, where they will have a place prepared for them by God - most likely the ancient stone city of Petra in Jordan.

Faithful Jews will flee from Israel. Rev 12:6, 14-17.

And John saw that the Messianic Jews that flee with them, will then feed New Testament Truth to these Jews in Petra for forty-two Jewish or 30 day months - the second half of the global trial and tribulation to come. These Jews will flee Jerusalem when the Antichrist's image is set in the rebuilt Jewish temple in Jerusalem, despite Satan's efforts to corrupt them.

Summary of Satan's Campaign against Faithful Jews

See Chart, Image 30 & 31

John then saw that there was war in heaven while the Lord Jesus Christ was ministering on earth between 26 AD and 29 AD. The archangel Michael and his holy angels fought against Satan and his fallen angels. And Michael and the holy angels prevailed, and cast Satan and the fallen angels out of heaven down to earth.

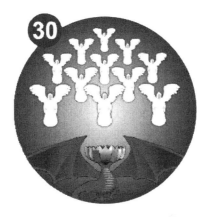

There was war in heaven while Christ was on earth. Rev 12:7-8.

And an authoritative voice in heaven then declared that salvation, strength, God's kingdom, and the authority of Christ, had all now become available to those who accepted Christ as Saviour, because Satan had now been cast out of heaven.

Jews were then therefore able to overcome Satan's tempting of them, by trusting in Christ's blood and in their testimony that Christ is the righteousness of God. And they no longer loved doing their own self-centered will.

And the holy angels in heaven following Satan's casting out, said, Woe to the people on earth, both Jew and Gentile! For the devil is come down unto you, having great wrath, because he knows that he has only a short time to conquer the world before Christ returns to overthrow him.

Satan and a third of the angels were cast down to Earth. Rev 12:9-13.

And John then saw that Satan began to persecute the nation of Israel as soon as he was cast out of heaven down to earth. Jerusalem and most of the Jews were destroyed by the Roman Empire in 70 AD. And those Jews who managed to escape, and their descendants, have been persecuted throughout the world ever since.

But after almost 2,000 years of persecution, God will deliver His wife - the nation of Israel - from Satan's persecution, most likely into the ancient stone city of Petra in Jordan. And Messianic Jews delivered with them, will then feed New Testament Truth to these Jews in Petra for forty-two Jewish or 30 day months - the second half of the global trial and tribulation to come.

And Satan will stir a flood of protest against the Jews in Petra, in an attempt to have them removed. But the Jews still in Israel will help the Jews in Petra, by swallowing up the flood of protest.

So Satan will go full out war against the rest of the Messianic Jews throughout the world, who keep the commandments of God, and testify that Jesus Christ is the promised Saviour.

Summary of the Antichrist's Campaign against Faithful Christians

See Chart, Image 32

John then found himself standing upon the fringe of the Gentile - or non-Jewish - nations, watching the demon king Apollyon rise to power out of the Gentile nations, in possession of a Gentile leader. This demon possessed Gentile leader will be the Antichrist. And he will rule the world via the ten most prominent countries into which the last of the seven kingdoms and empires of man will ultimately divide.

A Gentile leader will rule the world and become the Antichrist. Rev 13:1-10.

This demon king Apollyon is the agent by which Satan has been endeavouring to rule the world via the kingdoms and empires of Sumer, Egypt, Assyria, Babylon, Persia, Greece, and Rome. And he is the agent by which Satan will eventually rule the world via the ten most prominent countries into which the Roman Empire will ultimately divide - most likely, Britain, France, Germany, Italy, Spain, Greece, Turkey, Egypt, Iraq, and Iran.

And John saw that the Antichrist will come out of one of the countries that now constitute what was the Greek Empire, i.e. Greece, Turkey, Egypt, Iraq, Iran and Syria. He will trample the world under his feet, as the Persian Empire did. He will make a decree that all who refuse to worship his image be put to death, as the king of the Babylonian Empire did. And Satan will give him his ability to work miracles, his position of rule over the world, and also great authority.

And John saw that the last empire of man looked as if it was destroyed through war, and yet it will be restored again. And the world will admire and be amazed at the Antichrist, for he will restore the last empire of man - the Roman Empire - and will assume its sovereignty. And he will do it by subduing the leaders of three countries in Eastern Europe that are totally opposed to being united with Western Europe.

The Roman Empire appeared to be destroyed through war over 1500 years ago, yet its restoration as the European Union has been underway since 1948. The ten most prominent countries of the European Union will most likely be Britain, France, Germany, Italy, Spain, Greece, Turkey, Egypt, Iraq, and Iran. And the three countries that the Antichrist will subdue and unite with Western Europe are most likely Egypt, Iran and Iraq. A feat which would certainly cause the world to admire and be amazed at the Antichrist.

And the unrepentant world will worship Satan, who will empower the demon king Apollyon in possession of the Antichrist. And they will worship the Antichrist, saying, Who is like unto the beast? Who is able to make war with him - the great peace maker?

The Antichrist will most likely be a Pope of Rome possessed by the demon Apollyon, because the Pope has remained the indeposable leader of the Roman Empire for over 1500 years. All Catholics still officially become Roman citizens upon baptism. And Catholicism is the only religion besides Islam accepted by the citizens of Egypt, Iraq, and Iran, which the Antichrist will have to subdue.

And God will allow the Antichrist to speak boastful things and blasphemies, and to kill faithful Christians and Jews, for three and a half years - the second half of the global trial and tribulation to come.

And the Antichrist will speak irreverently against Jesus Christ, the heavenly temple, and the faithful Christians miraculously caught up to the heavenly temple at the end of the Church Age. And God will allow him to make war with the Christians and Jews left on earth who, in response to the trial and tribulation of the first four seals, repent and become faithful to Christ. The Antichrist will be allowed to kill them, and thereby deliver them to heaven. He will be given authority over the entire world via the ten most prominent countries of the restored Roman Empire, for the entire second half of the global trial and tribulation.

And all the unrepentant will worship the Antichrist as the saviour of the world, during the second half of the global trial and tribulation to come. For God will send them strong delusion so that they will believe the Antichrist's lies.

If anyone has a spiritual ear, let him hear this: Every unfaithful Christian and Jew who repents and becomes righteous by imprisoning their thoughts to the obedience of Christ, and holy by killing their worldly desires through faith in Christ, during the coming global trial and tribulation, will be imprisoned and killed by the Antichrist in order to prove their endurance in the Christian faith and their faithfulness to Christ.

Note that the Antichrist will rule the entire world as the leader of the European Union unopposed by America or Russia. This is primarily because Russia will have been crippled just prior to the global trial and tribulation by the Gog and Mogog war prophesied in Ezekiel 38. And America will have been crippled by the catching up to heaven of its faithful Christians prior to the global trial and tribulation, and also by the death of its repentant unfaithful Christians under the fourth seal.

Summary of the False Prophet's Deception of Unfaithful Jews

See Chart, Image 33 & 34

John then took special note as he watched another demon rise to power, this time out of the Israeli nation, in possession of a Jewish leader. This demon possessed Jewish leader will be the False Prophet. He will have both religious and political authority, like Christ has. And he will corrupt peoples' minds from the simplicity that is in God's Word, like Satan does.

A Jewish leader will unite with the Antichrist. Rev 13:11-13.

This False Prophet will exercise all the Antichrist's power. And he will cause the Jews who remain in Israel to worship the Antichrist. He will do great wonders, making fire come down from the sky onto the earth for the whole world to see. And he will deceive Jews throughout the entire world, by means of those miracles which he will do on behalf of the Antichrist.

And he will tell the Jews in Israel to make an image to the Antichrist, and to set it in the rebuilt Jewish temple in

Jerusalem. He will then give life to the image, so that it will speak and cause those who refuse to worship the Antichrist to be killed by the sword.

The Antichrist's image will be placed in the rebuilt Jewish temple. Rev 13:14-18.

And he will cause the unrepentant of every class of people throughout the entire world to receive a microchip implant into their right hand or into their forehead. And no one will be able to buy or sell anything unless they have the Antichrist's microchip implant, containing the Antichrist's name and the number of his name.

Here is wisdom. Let him that has understanding count the number of this False Prophet. For it is the number of a man. And this man's number will be six hundred and sixty six.

Summary of Christ's Catching-Up to Heaven of the Sealed Jews

See Chart, Image 35

John then saw that the Lord Jesus Christ will stand on mount Zion at Jerusalem, with the 144,000 sealed of the Messianic Jews. And from out of heaven will come the testimony of the caught up to heaven Church, that Christ's gospel concerning His kingdom is the power of God unto salvation.

Then the 144,000 sealed Messianic Jews will be caught up to heaven. And they will sing a new song, before the throne of reconciliation, before the four beasts, and before the elders of the caught up to heaven Church. And no one but them will be able to sing that song. For they will be the first members of Israel to enter heaven, a token body of all faithful Old Testament believers yet to be resurrected.

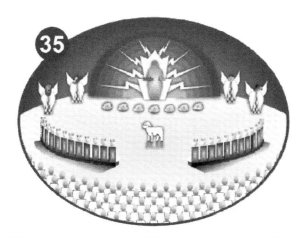

The 144,000 sealed Messianic Jews will be caught-up to heaven. Rev 14:1-5.

These Messianic Jews will stand before the throne of reconciliation in heaven, because they believed Christ's gospel of His kingdom, and were evaluated during their life as being gracious at heart: holy.

Summary of the Final Call to the World for Repentance

See Chart, Image 36

John then saw that another angel will fly across the sky, having the everlasting gospel to preach unto all who are still dwelling on the earth just before the outpouring of God's wrath. And this angel will command the world to fear and glorify God, because the time of global judgment has come.

And another angel will follow, declaring that Babylon has fallen, because it caused all nations to suffer the consequences of its joining divine revelation with false religious beliefs.

And yet another angel will follow, declaring with authority that all who will worship the Antichrist and his image, and receive his mark in their forehead or hand, will suffer the impending wrath of God, followed by eternal torment in the lake of fire.

There will be a final call to the world to repent. Rev 14:6-13.

John then heard a voice from heaven telling him to write: Endowed with God's favour are those who obey Jehovah and have faith in Christ i.e. Messianic Jews throughout the world, who die from this point onwards in this Revelation. For in doing so they will not suffer the impending wrath of God. Rather, they will in death receive rest from their labours, followed by resurrection to eternal glory on the new earth to come.

Summary of the Gathering of the World's Armies against the Israeli Nation

See Chart, Image 37

John then saw - take special note - that the Lord Jesus Christ's angelic representative will come down again from heaven, clothed with Christ's majesty and strength, bearing Christ's full authority, and holding a sharp sickle in his hand.

And another angel will come out of the temple in heaven, and will instruct the Lord Jesus Christ's angelic representative to thrust his sickle into the world and reap the unrepentant non-Christian nations of Eastern Europe, for their wickedness has come to fruition.

And the Lord's representative angel will then thrust his sickle into the world on behalf of Christ, and will gather the armies of the unrepentant non-Christian nations together into the valley of Armageddon, just north of Jerusalem.

Then another angel with a sickle will come out of the temple in heaven.

*The armies of the world will be gathered
to Armageddon. Rev 14:14-20.*

And another angel will come out from the altar of martyred believers in heaven, bearing authority concerning God's wrath. And this angel will instruct the angel with the second sickle to thrust his sickle into the world and reap the unrepentant Christian nations of Western Europe, for their wickedness is fully ripe.

And the angel with the second sickle will then thrust his sickle into the world, and will gather the armies of the unrepentant Christian nations together also into the valley of Armageddon, into the great bloodbath of God's wrath. And the blood shed will begin just outside Jerusalem, and will extend for approximately two hundred miles.

Chapter Four

THINGS YET FUTURE, CONTINUED

Revelation 15:1-8; 16:1-21.

The Seventh Trumpet, Continued

John then saw that when the seventh angel sounds his trumpet, another seven angels will stand in heaven bearing the final seven plagues.

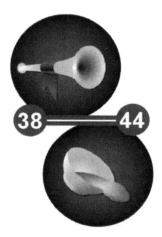

The seven vials of God's wrath. Rev 15:1-8; 16:2-21.

And all those of the five unfaithful churches who repent and become faithful to Christ during the coming global trial and tribulation, and all Jews who do the same, who are therefore martyred by the Antichrist for refusing to worship him and take his mark, will stand upon the sea of glass mingled with fire before the throne of reconciliation in heaven, which symbolizes their redemption through trial and tribulation. And they will sing the song of Moses and the song of Christ, declaring that Christ is both the saviour and also a man of war, and that His ways are just and true, and that He alone is inherently holy and therefore worthy to judge the world of their worldliness, their un-holiness.

Then - take special note - the temple of testimony will open within heaven. And out of the temple will come seven angels, bearing the final seven plagues. They will be clothed as representatives of Christ in pure and white linen.

And one of the four beasts will give these seven angels seven golden vials full of the wrath of God. And the temple in heaven will fill with smoke from the glory of God, and from his power. And no mere human will be able to enter the temple until the seven plagues of God's wrath are fulfilled.

Then the Lord Jesus Christ from within the temple will command these seven angels to go and pour out the vials of God's wrath upon the entire unrepentant world.

The First Six Vials

See Chart, Images 38-43

The first angel will then pour out his vial upon the Israeli nation, and grievous sores will befall those Jews who will have the mark of the Antichrist, and who worship his image set in the rebuilt Jewish temple.

The second angel will then pour out his vial upon the Gentile - or non-Jewish - nations, and all the unrepentant of the five unfaithful churches will die spiritually, becoming void of what Spirit of Truth they had.

The third angel will then pour out his vial upon all the false religious teachers, and their false teaching will become repugnant to them.

And this third angel will declare that Christ is righteous to judge false religious teachers, by causing them to ingest repugnant teaching. For they cause the death of faithful Christians. And another angel from the altar of martyred believers will also declare that Christ is righteous in His judgment.

The fourth angel will then pour out his vial upon the sun, and the entire unrepentant world will be scorched with great heat. They will blaspheme the Lord Jesus Christ for sending these plagues. And they will refuse to repent of their works and give Him glory.

The fifth angel will then pour out his vial upon the power base of the Antichrist, and all who worship him will be tormented. They will gnaw their tongues because of the pain. They also will blaspheme the Lord Jesus Christ for sending this plague. And they also will refuse to repent of their works.

The sixth angel will then pour out his vial upon the great river Euphrates, and its water will be dried up so that the leaders of the unrepentant non-Christian nations of Eastern Europe can journey across dry land to Jerusalem for the battle of Armageddon.

Christ's Warning to Christians Now Concerning the Day of Wrath

John then saw that three unholy spirits - one from the devil, one from the Antichrist, and one from the Israeli false prophet - will go forth working miracles to the rulers of the unrepentant world, to gather them to the battle of that great day of God Almighty.

Take special note, I the Lord Jesus Christ will at the battle of Armageddon suddenly come upon those in doctrinal ignorance. Endowed with God's favour are those who stand doctrinally vigilant, and keep their God-given robe of righteousness, so that they are not naked and ashamed when I return at Armageddon.

And it is actually the Lord Jesus Christ who gathers the unrepentant world to Armageddon, because He is God Almighty, and all things are therefore done in accordance with His will.

The Seventh Vial

See Chart, Image 44

The seventh angel will then pour out his vial into the air. And Christ from His throne in the heavenly temple will say, It is done. For the outpouring of the seventh vial is the completion of the sounding of the seven trumpets - the assertion of Christ's complete authority over His creation. And the kingdoms of the world will become the kingdoms of God in heaven and of Christ: God incarnate. And Christ will then reign for ever and ever over all earthly kingdoms, beginning on this present earth for a millennium, and continuing on the new earth to come for all eternity.

And out of the temple and the throne of reconciliation will come voices, thunders, and lightnings. And upon the earth will be the greatest earthquake ever. Jerusalem will be divided into three parts. All the cities of the Gentile nations will be devastated, especially Babylon. And both the subordinate and the most dominant kingdoms of the world will be destroyed. A great hail out of heaven will fall upon the entire unrepentant world, every stone about 25 kilograms. And the world will blaspheme the Lord Jesus Christ because of the plague of hail.

Continued on page 74, at Revelation 18:1.

Chapter Five

THIRD INFORMATIVE INTERLUDE

Revelation 17:1-18.

The Mother of all False Religions and Idolatry

See Chart, Image 45

One of the seven angels that had the seven vials of God's wrath then told John to come with him, and that he would show him the judgment of the great whore that sits upon many waters, with whom the rulers of the earth have fornicated, and the inhabitants of the earth have been made incapable of sober spiritual judgment due to the product of her joining divine revelation with false religious beliefs.

And the angel carried John away in the spirit into the wilderness, and showed him a woman sitting on a scarlet coloured beast, a beast full of names of blasphemy, with seven heads and ten horns. The woman was dressed in purple and scarlet priestly garments, decked with righteous works. Bearing a religious testimony and testament. And holding a cup full of her pride and fornication. And on her forehead was written the name, MYSTERY, BABYLON THE GREAT, THE MOTHER OF HARLOTS AND ABOMINATIONS OF THE EARTH. For she is the mother of all false religions and idolatry.

The spirit of Babylon is reigning off the back of the demon Apollyon. Rev 17:1-18.

John saw that the woman was intoxicated with the blood of martyred Jews and Christians. And John wondered with great admiration for the woman. So the angel asked John why he marveled at her. And then proceeded to set him straight concerning her identity and that of the scarlet beast which carries her.

The scarlet beast reigned on earth in the past in possession of human rulers. But was not reigning at the time of the giving of this Revelation. Yet will in the future ascend out of the bottomless pit to again reign on earth in possession of another human ruler. This scarlet beast is the demon king Apollyon, and his destiny is eternal damnation. And the unrepentant world will wonder after him, when he reigns in the future.

The seven heads on the scarlet beast are the seven most dominant consecutive kingdoms and empires of man, upon which the woman resides spiritually i.e. Sumeria, Egypt, Assyria, Babylon, Persia, Greece and Rome.

And there are seven key human kings and emperors. At the time of the giving of this Revelation, the first five have fallen, the sixth is in power, and the seventh is yet to come. When the seventh comes to power, he will continue for a mere forty-two months - the second half of the global trial and tribulation to come. The first five key human kings and emperors were most likely Ramses of Egypt, Pul, Shalmaneser and Sennacherib of Assyria, and Nebuchadnezzar of Babylon. The sixth was Domitian of Rome. And the seventh will be the Antichrist of the restored Roman Empire - the leader of the European Union.

The scarlet beast is the eighth king: the demon king Apollyon. He is of the seven key human kings, in that he is the ruler of them all on behalf of Satan. And his destiny is eternal damnation.

The ten horns on the scarlet beast are the rulers of the ten most prominent countries of the restored Roman Empire, the European Union i.e. Britain, France, Germany, Italy, Spain, Greece, Turkey, Egypt, Iraq, and Iran. At the time of the giving of this Revelation they had not yet come to be. They will reign under the Antichrist during the coming global trial and tribulation.

These ten rulers will unite, and will give their power and strength to the Antichrist, by whom Satan will finally rule the entire world. And they and the Antichrist will then fight against the Lord Jesus Christ, at the battle of Armageddon. But Christ will overcome them, because He is Lord of lords, and King of kings. And those who will be with Christ at the battle of Armageddon are divinely called, chosen, and faithful to Him.

And the waters upon which the woman sits, are all the citizens of the kingdoms and empires of man.

The rulers of the ten most prominent countries of the restored Roman Empire will hate the woman. They will expose her unrighteousness. And will burn her with fire at the onset of the battle of Armageddon. For God has put it in their hearts to fulfil his will, and to agree and give their confederate kingdom unto the Antichrist, until all Bible prophecy concerning the

Antichrist is fulfilled.

And the woman - the great whore - is the spirit of the great city Babel or Babylon, the mother of all false religions and idolatry, who reigns spiritually over the rulers of the earth, off the back of the demon king Apollyon as he influences all seven most dominant consecutive kingdoms and empires of man. This spirit of Babel or Babylon is the spirit of false religion and idolatry. It spread throughout the world from the tower of Babel, embodied in the goddess Ishtar, Isis, Aphrodite, Venus, Diana, and most recently in the Virgin Mary. This is the great whore known as the queen of heaven. Jer 7:18.

Chapter Six

THINGS YET FUTURE, CONCLUDED

Revelation 18:1-24; 19:1-21; 20:1-15; 21:1-8.

The Judgment of the Great Whore

See Chart, Image 46

John then saw another angel come down from heaven, having great authority; and the earth was lightened with his glory. And the angel cried mightily with authority, saying, Babylon the great is fallen, is fallen, and has become the habitation of all religious deceivers, and the hold of every unbelieving soul, and a cage of every unclean and hateful believer. For all nations have partaken of the fruit of her joining divine revelation with false religious beliefs, and the rulers of the earth have fornicated with her, and the world's traders of religious merchandise are waxed rich through the abundance of her delicacies.

Then John heard the voice of Christ from out of heaven, saying to Christians now, Abandon her, my people, so that you do not participate in her unrighteous works, and consequently suffer God's judgment upon her. For her unrighteous works have reached unto heaven, and God has remembered her iniquities. Reward her with spiritual desolation, as she rewarded so many Christians with spiritual desolation. And endorse God's wrath upon her according to her works. How much she has glorified herself, and has lived deliciously. Give her so much torment and sorrow by abandoning her. For she says in her heart, I sit a queen - the queen of heaven - and am no widow, and will see no sorrow.

Therefore God's judgment upon her will come in one day:

Plagues of spiritual death, of mourning, of famine, and of destruction by fire. For strong is the Lord God who judges her. And the rulers of the earth, who have fornicated and lived deliciously with her, will bewail her, and lament for her, when they see the smoke of her burning. Standing afar off for fear of sharing her torment, they will say, Alas, alas that great city Babylon, that mighty city! For in one hour your judgment has come.

The spirit of Babylon will be destroyed. Rev 18:1-24.

And the world's traders of religious merchandise will weep and mourn over her. For no man will any longer be able to buy their religious merchandise, their merchandise of religious works, testimony, testament, outward righteousness, priestly garments, building material, containers, incense, wine, oil, bread, meat, ceremonial transportation, loyal subjects, and souls of men. And the fruits of her joining divine revelation with false religious beliefs that men lusted after i.e. worldly gratification, are departed from them. And all things which were dainty and godly are departed from them, never to be found again.

And the traders of her merchandise, who were made rich by her, will weep and wail. Standing afar off for fear of sharing her torment, they will say, Alas, alas that great city Babylon, which was clothed in priestly garments of purple and scarlet, and was decked with gold, precious stones, and pearls! For in one hour so great riches will have come to nothing.

And every religious leader, and all the members of religious organizations, and all the staff of religious organizations, and as many as trade via the religious realm, will stand afar off, and will cry when they see the smoke of her burning, saying, What city is like unto this great city! And they will cast dust on their heads, and cry, weeping and wailing, saying, Alas, alas that great city, by which everyone in religious organizations where made rich through selling her merchandise! For in one hour she has been made desolate.

Rejoice over her, all you in heaven, and all faithful ministers of God's Word who were martyred at her hand. For God has avenged you on her.

And a mighty angel will then take up a stone like a great millstone, and will cast it into the sea, saying, Thus with violence will that great city Babylon be thrown down, never to be found again. No religious music will be heard again in her. No craftsman such as jewellers or tailors, who make religious clothing, will be found again in her. No sound of a millstone grinding wheat for religious food will be heard again in her. The testament to the righteousness of God will never shine again in her. And the testimony of the Lord Jesus Christ and of His bride - the Church - will never be heard again in her. For although her traders were the most prominent religious leaders of the world, all the nations were deceived by her perceived supernatural practices. But not anymore.

And in her was found the blood of divinely inspired ministers of God's Word, and of faithful conveyers of God's Word, and of all martyred Jews and Christians.

The Marriage of Christ with all Faithful Christians

John then saw that all the caught-up to heaven Church will then worship God, saying, Hallelujah! Salvation, glory, honour, and authority, unto the Lord our God. For true and righteous are his judgments. For by destroying Babylon, He has judged the spirit of Babel and Babylon - the spirit of false religion and idolatry - which corrupted the earth with her joining divine revelation with false religious beliefs. And God has avenged the blood of all the Jews and Christians who were killed by her. And again the caught-up Church will say, Alleluia! And Babylon's smoke will rise up for ever and ever.

Then the twenty four elders of the caught-up Church, and the four beasts, will fall down and worship God that sits on the throne of reconciliation, saying, Amen and Alleluia. Thereby declaring their agreement of God's judgment upon Babylon.

Then a voice will come out of the throne, saying, Praise our God, all you faithful Christians, and you that fear him, both small and great. And the voice of a great congregation, as the testimony of many peoples, multitudes, nations and tongues, and as the authority of God, will respond by saying, Alleluia! Thereby declaring their adoration for the Lord Jesus Christ as He finally exercises His complete and absolute rule over His creation. And they will say, Let us be glad and rejoice, and give honour to Him. For the marriage of the Lord Jesus Christ has come, and his wife - the caught-up Church - has made herself ready, in that her members have overcome their worldliness through faith in Him as the righteousness of God. And they all will then be dressed in fine linen - their God given robes of righteousness. Whereas those professing Christians still on earth will be naked and ashamed when Christ returns at Armageddon.

The angel that showed John the judgment of the great whore, then told him to write, Endowed with God's favour are those who are called to participate in the marriage supper of Christ - the battle of Armageddon - on Christ's side. And the angel said, These are the true sayings of God.

Moved with gratitude as one of those endowed with God's favour, John fell at the angel's feet to worship him. But the angel told John not to worship him, because he is merely a fellow servant of God, bearing Christ's testimony. The angel told John to worship only God, because only God's Word contains the spirit of divine revelation. As opposed to the word of any human or angelic being.

The Marriage Supper of Christ

See Chart, Image 47 & 48

John then saw that heaven will then open, and - take special note - the Lord Jesus Christ will come out of heaven and down to earth to personally conquer the world, and thereby complete God's wrath upon the unrepentant world, and also physically establish His eternal kingdom. Christ is called Faithful and True, and will judge and make war righteously. He is the instrument of God's vengeance. He has complete authority over all humanity. He will bear an unrevealed name - the name of God. His clothing will be dipped in the blood of those gathered against Him at the battle of Armageddon. And His name is The Word of God.

The armies of heaven, both angelic and Christian, will follow Christ out of heaven and down to earth, in the spirit of conquest, clothed in their undefiled God given robes of righteousness.

Christ will return and conquer the world. Rev 19:11-21.

Christ will then smite the unrepentant nations with the righteous judgment of His words at the battle of Armageddon. And He will rule with a rod of iron for a millennium over all those who remain on the earth after the battle. He will tread the winepress of the fierceness and wrath of Almighty God. And on His clothing and on His thigh will be written, KING OF KINGS, AND LORD OF LORDS.

And an angel standing in the righteousness of God, will cry with authority to the faithful Jews throughout the world, saying, Come and gather yourselves together unto the marriage supper of the great God: the battle of Armageddon. Come and devour the flesh of all those gathered for war against the Israeli nation.

And the demon king Apollyon in possession of the Antichrist, and the kings of the earth along with their armies, will all gather together for the battle of Armageddon, to make war against Israel, against the Lord Jesus Christ, and against his army of angels and faithful Christians.

The armies of the world will gather
against Christ. Rev 19:19-21.

And the Antichrist and the Israeli false prophet will be taken and cast alive into the lake of fire burning with brimstone. And the kings of the earth and their armies will be killed by the righteous judgment of God out of Christ's mouth. And the faithful Jews from throughout the world will return to Jerusalem and have their fill of their enemies' flesh.

The Binding of Satan for a Thousand Years

See Chart, Image 49

John then saw that an angel will then come down from heaven, having a great chain in his hand, and also the key to the bottomless pit, where the demon king Apollyon is bound when not in possession of human rulers. And the angel will take Satan, and will bind him, and cast him into the bottomless pit, and seal him in for a thousand years, so that he cannot deceive the nations again until the end of Christ's millennial reign on earth.

Satan will be bound for a thousand years. Rev 20:1-3.

The Restoration of the Kingdom of God

See Chart, Image 50

Thrones will then be set. And on these thrones will sit all the faithful Christians of the Church Age, caught-up to heaven just before the global trial and tribulation. And all the 144,000 sealed of the Messianic Jews, caught-up to heaven just before the outpouring of God's wrath at the end of the global trial and tribulation. Also there, will be the souls of all the unfaithful Christians who repent and become faithful to Christ unto death at the hands of the Antichrist during the global trial and tribulation. And they will all live and rule in immortality from Jerusalem with Christ over what remains of the nations after Armageddon, for a thousand years in the restored kingdom of God on earth.

The faithful will reign on earth with Christ for a thousand years. Rev 20:4-6.

But everyone else who will have ever died, will remain dead until the end of Christ's thousand year reign on earth.

This life and reign in immortality with Christ for a millennium is the first resurrection - the first resurrected state or afterlife. Endowed with God's favour, and holy, are everyone who has part in the first resurrection. Therefore eternal condemnation in the lake of fire will be of no concern to them, unlike what remains of the nations after Armageddon, who will later rebel and therefore be condemned.

Everyone who has part in the first resurrection will be priests of God and of Christ - God incarnate - and will reign from Jerusalem with Christ for a thousand years in the restored Kingdom of God on earth.

The Final Rebellion of Humanity

See Chart, Image 51

At the end of Christ's thousand year reign on earth, Satan will be set free for a season. He will immediately deceive the repopulated nations, and gather them together for battle. And the nations, repopulated in Europe, Africa, and north and south Asia, will travel across the land, and will besiege the camp of God's people, and the city of Jerusalem. But fire will come down from God out of heaven, and will devour them.

The nations of the world will gather against Christ. Rev 20:7-9.

The Ultimate Destiny of Satan and All Humanity

See Chart, Images 52-54

Satan will then be cast into the lake of fire and brimstone, to join the Antichrist and the Israeli false prophet in continual and never ending torment.

Satan will be cast into the lake of fire. Rev 20:10.

The Lord Jesus Christ - the Word of God and supreme authority - will then sit upon a great white throne. And the present heaven and earth will be burned up, and will melt away.

Christ will judge the dead. Rev 20:11-15.

Those who were just devoured by fire from God out of heaven will then stand before Christ: God incarnate. And the books which contain the history of every deed done by every person will be opened. And the book of life, which contains the names of every faithful servant of God, that is, all those who have lived in accordance with God's will as opposed to their own. And those who were just devoured by fire from God out of heaven will be judged according to their deeds recorded in the books.

Then all the dead faithful servants of God will be resurrected out of the sea of redemption. Then all the unrepentant unfaithful servants of God will be resurrected out of death. And then all unbelievers will be resurrected out of hell. And they will all be judged according to their works recorded in the books.

Death and hell, and whoever is not found written in the book of life, will then be cast into the lake of fire, which is the second death.

A new heaven and a new earth will then be created. And the new and holy city of Jerusalem will come down onto the new earth from God out of heaven, prepared as a bride adorned for her husband.

A new heaven and earth will be created. Rev 21:1-8.

And - take special note - a great voice out of heaven will say, the tabernacle of God is now with humans, and God will dwell with them, and they will be His people, and God Himself will be with them and be their God for evermore. And God will wipe away all tears from their eyes. And there will be no more death, no more sorrow, no more crying, and no more pain. For the former things are passed away.

And Christ, God incarnate, sitting on the great white throne, will then say, Behold, I make all things new.

Christ then spoke to John, and told him to write His following declaration, because His words are true and faithful:

Christ then declared: It is done. I, the Lord Jesus Christ, am the one and only true God and Savior, the author of salvation from creation through to eternity. I will freely give the water of eternal life to whoever really thirsts for it. Whoever overcomes their worldliness will inherit all things. And I will be their God. And they will be my son. But the fearful, and unbelieving, and the abominable, and murderers, and whoremongers, and sorcerers, and idolaters, and all liars, will have their part in the lake which burns with fire and brimstone: the second death.

Chapter Seven

FOURTH INFORMATIVE INTERLUDE

Revelation 21:9-27; 22:1-5.

The New Jerusalem

One of the seven angels that had the seven vials of God's wrath then told John to come with him, and that he would show John Christ's wife, the Church - body of faithful Christians built together for God to inhabit. And the angel carried John away in the spirit, to a great and high mountain, and showed him that great city, the new holy Jerusalem, descending down to the new earth, out of heaven from God.

John saw that the new city of Jerusalem will have God's glory, and that it will shine like a most precious stone, like a jasper, as clear as crystal. It will have a great and high wall, with twelve gateways, each named after one of the twelve tribes of Israel. And it will have an angel at each gate, to control who enters the city. For no one may enter except the nation of Israel, of which all faithful Christians have been made fellow citizens. Eph 2:19.

The city wall will have four sides, with three of its twelve gates on each side. And it will have twelve foundations, each named after one of the twelve apostles. For the Church - body of faithful Christians - is built squarely upon the doctrine of the twelve apostles, the teaching that Jesus Christ is both Saviour and Lord, and therefore must be both trusted and obeyed.

The angel that showed John the city, then measured it, its gates, and its wall. The city will be cube shaped, approximately 1,400 miles high and wide. And its wall will be approximately 200 feet thick.

The wall will be made of jasper, symbolizing the holiness required to enter. The city within will be made of gold, symbolizing the righteous works of God's faithful servants. The twelve foundations of the wall will each be made of a precious stone, symbolizing the faithful testimony of each of the apostles. And the twelve gates will each be a single pearl, symbolizing the faithful testament of each of the twelve tribes of Israel.

John saw that the city will not have a physical temple. For the Lord God Almighty and Christ - God incarnate - will be its temple. The city will not need the light of the sun, which represents God's Word: the definition of righteousness. Nor will it need the light of the moon, which represents God's law: the definition of unrighteousness. For God's glory will lighten it, and Christ - God's Word - will be its light.

The new nations of saved people will live in the light of the city. For there will be no sun or moon. The kings of the new nations will bring their glory and honour into the city. Its gates will never shut. For there will be no night. And no one unholy will enter the city. No one that defiles, or causes abomination, or makes a lie. Only those whose names are written in Christ's book of life i.e. those who do God's will, as opposed to their own.

The angel that showed John the city, then showed him that a river of the water of eternal spiritual life will proceed out of God's throne in the city. And in the middle of the city street, and on either side of the river, there will be the tree of eternal physical life, which will bear twelve types of fruit every month. And its leaves will be for the perpetual bodily healing of the nations. Therefore there will be no more curse of death. Instead, God's throne will be on the new earth in the new city, with the people, and God's faithful servants will serve him forever. And they will see the Lord Jesus Christ's face, and his name will be in their foreheads.

There will not be doctrinal ignorance there. The people will not need a testimony to Christ's righteousness, or a light of understanding concerning God's will. For the Lord God will personally enlighten them. And they will reign with Him for ever and ever.

Conclusion

SUMMARY OF CHRIST'S REVELATION

Revelation 22:6-21.

The angel then told John that this Revelation is faithful and true, and that the Lord Jesus Christ sent it via His representative angel, to show his servants - Christians - the global trial and tribulation that must abruptly come upon the world.

Christ then said to take special note that He will come upon those in doctrinal ignorance, unexpectedly like a thief comes in the night, at the end of the global trial and tribulation. Endowed with God's favour are those who comply with Christ's message in this Revelation to Christians. For only those who faithfully abide by Christ's word are sure to be kept from this global trial and tribulation.

Moved by all that he had seen and heard, John again fell at the angel's feet to worship him. But the angel again told John not to worship him, because he is merely a fellow servant of God, bearing Christ's testimony, and submissive to God's will. The angel again told John to worship only God. For only God's Word contains the spirit of divine revelation. As opposed to the word of any human or angelic being.

The angel then told John not to seal up this Revelation, because the global trial and tribulation is near.

Whoever is unjust, in that they are good only towards those who are good towards them, keep it up, and you will get a just reward. Whoever is filthy, in that they are self-indulgent, materialistic, or self-important, keep it up, and you will get a just reward.

And whoever is righteous, in that they do to others as they would have others do to them, irrespective of persons, keep it up, and you will get a just reward. And whoever is holy, in that they overcome their self-indulgence, materialism, and self-importance, keep it up, and you will get a just reward.

Take special note, the Lord Jesus Christ will come upon unfaithful Christians, unexpectedly as a thief comes in the night, at the end the global trial and tribulation. And He will bring with Him just reward for everyone according to their works. The unjust and unholy will receive eternal condemnation in the lake of fire. Whereas the righteous and holy will receive eternal life and glory on the new earth to come.

I am the author of salvation from creation through to eternity, says the Lord Jesus Christ, the eternal God, the Almighty.

Endowed with God's favour are those who abide in Christ's doctrine, in that they do to others as they would have others do to them irrespective of persons, and they overcome self-indulgence, materialism, and self-importance. They will have right to the tree of eternal physical life. And they will enter into the new city of Jerusalem, and into eternal spiritual life.

For no one unrighteous or unholy will enter the city. No one who adamantly voices their own definition of righteousness, or uses perceived supernatural powers to deceive, or has dealings with false religion, or has part in the death of faithful Christians, or who worships idols, or enjoys and fabricates lies - No one who does any of these things will be rewarded eternal life.

I have sent My angel to convey this Revelation to you in the seven types of churches within Christendom. I am the root and the offspring of King David, and I am the supreme authority, says the Lord Jesus Christ.

And the Spirit of eternal life and the New Jerusalem, invite you. And let whoever understands, invite others. And let whoever really thirsts for the water of eternal life, come and receive it. And whosoever will come and receive it, let them do so unhindered. For the Lord Jesus Christ testifies to all who hear this Revelation, that if anyone causes a hindrance by adding more prophecy to it, God will send upon them the plagues that are written in this book. And if anyone causes a hindrance by detracting from the significance of this Revelation, God will take away their part out of the book of eternal life, and out of the holy new city of Jerusalem, and from all the good things that are written in this book.

The Lord Jesus Christ says that He will surely come upon those in doctrinal ignorance, unexpectedly like a thief in the night, at the end of the global trial and tribulation to come. Amen. Even so, come, Lord Jesus.

May the Spirit of graciousness from our Lord Jesus Christ be with you all. Amen.

CHART

Get your copy of the giant full colour companion chart...

Via download from: https://flic.kr/s/aHsm4jYtR3
Or,
Via email from: witback @ gmail.com

See the following seven piece sample copy. The actual chart, via download or email, comes in seven high resolution A4 size printer friendly pieces.

Please post a positive review of this book and chart on Amazon. Reviews are very important. So please take the time to post one. Thank You.

REVELATION

Rev 12:7-8.
WAR IN HEAVEN
DURING CHRIST'S
MINISTRY ON EARTH

Rev 12:3-4.
SATAN REIGNING VIA THE SEVEN
DOMINANT KINGDOMS OF MAN
STANDING BEFORE THE ISRAELI NATION
TO DEVOUR CHRIST AT HIS BIRTH

ALL
CHU
CA
BEFORE
TR

Rev 12:5.
CHRIST CAUGHT-UP
TO HEAVEN AFTER
HIS RESURRECTION

30

27

Rev 12:1-2.
THE ISRAELI
NATION ABOUT
TO GIVE BIRTH
TO CHRIST

To the doctrinally d
Repent, or else Chri
God's household.

To the doctrinally v
Remain faithful to C
He will give you a c

To the doctrinally c
Repent, or else Chri
righteous judgment

To the doctrinally c
Repent, or else Chri
great tribulation & t

To the doctrinally n
Repent, or else Chri
unexpectedly like a

To the doctrinally v
Because you have k
will keep you from t

To the doctrinally a
Repent, or else Chri
God's household.

CREATION

KINGDOM OF SUMER

KINGDOM OF EGYPT

KINGDOM OF ASSYRIA

KINGDOM OF GOD

BYLON

MINISTRY

STAR

45

31

THE SPIRIT OF BABYLON &
THE DEMON KING APOLLYON
REIGNING ON BEHALF OF SATAN VIA
THE SEVEN DOMINANT KINGDOMS OF MAN
Rev 17:1-18.

SATAN & A THIRD
OF THE ANGELS
CAST OUT OF HEAVEN
DOWN TO EARTH
Rev 12:9-13.

C3974BC

SEVEN DOMINANT KINGDOMS OF
MAN & THE KINGDOM OF GOD

c26AD

PRESENT

CHRIST'S MES
OF CHURCHE

SAMPLE IMAGE

Rev 6:9-11.
SOULS OF THE REPENTANT
OF THE FIVE UNFAITHFUL
CHURCHES VINDICATED
IN HEAVEN

14

THIRD YEAR   FOURTH YEAR   FIFTH YEAR   SIXTH YEA

3   4   6

GLOBAL FOOD RATIONING

THE UNREPEN
ROUSED ON E

THE UNREPENTANT

THOSE KILLED BY SATAN
VINDICATED IN HE
INITIALLY WITH
OF R

13   15

AN EXECUTIVE
-GULATES GLOBAL
FOOD RATIONING
Rev 6:5-6

SATAN BEG
WHO RE
TH

THE GOSPE
CAUSES MOURI
THE MOSAIC L
BECOMES UNPAL
ALL PROPHE
HITS HOME
Rev 6:12-17

ISH FALSE PROPHET
TESTIFIES THAT THE
HRIST IS THE CHRIST
Rev 13:11-18.

33   666

25

JEWISH TRUE PROPHETS
TESTIFY THAT JESUS
IS THE CHRIST
Rev 11:3-13.

ANTICHRIST

NTICHRIST'S
MAGE IN THE
AELI TEMPLE
2 Thess 2:4;
13:5-8 & 14-15.

JERUSALEM

FAITHFUL JEWS
FLEE ISRAEL
TO PETRA
Rev 12:6 & 14-17.

34   32   29

Rev 13:1-10

SAMPLE IMAGE

AL & TRIBULATION: THREE & A HALF YEARS TRIAL OF THE FIVE UNFAITHFUL CHURC
LF YEARS OF GREAT TRIBULATION UPON THE ENTIRE UNREPENTANT WORLD   Dan 9:27; M

Rev 7:9-17.
ALL THE REPENTANT OF THE
FIVE UNFAITHFUL CHURCHES
CAUGHT-UP TO HEAVEN
BEFORE THE SEVENTH SEAL -
DAY OF GOD'S WRATH

17

Rev 14:1-5.
THE 144,000 SEALED JEWS
CAUGHT-UP TO HEAVEN
BEFORE THE SEVENTH
TRUMPET - OUTPOURING
OF GOD'S WRATH

35

:AR   **SEVENTH YEAR**

1 Thess 5:9; Rev 6:17.
THE DAY OF WRATH

THE DAY OF TH...

**NTANT
EARTH**

SE\
WITH THE SEV

18   **20**   **21**   **23**

THIRD OF   THIRD OF   IRE WORLD   THIR
TREES &   SEA LIFE   ORMENTED   THE W
ALL GRASS   &   [EXCEPT   KIL
BURNED UP   DE   E 144,000   Rev 9
Rev 8:7   LED JEWS]
                                               Rev 9:1-11.

EL
RNING.
: LAW
LATABLE.
IECY
ME
I?

16

144,00 JEWS SEALED
ON EARTH BEFORE
THE SEVENTH SEAL -
DAY OF GOD'S WRATH
Rev 7:1-8.

FAITHFUL JEWS IN PETRA

CHES

Matt 24:15-21.

The start of global trial and tribulation [c2019AD] is deduced as seven ye
on God's plan of salvation being composed of four millennia of preparat
God in His plan of creation, namely, four days of preparation for creation

THE THIRD HEAVEN: TEMPORY ABODE OF THOSE CAUGHT-UP

THE SEA OF REDEMPTION: TEMPORY ABODE OF DEAD FAITH

EVEN TRUMPETS ASSERT CHRIST
EVENTH POURING OUT

IIRD OF
WORLD
ILLED
9:13-21.

38   39   40   43

UNREPENTANT   UNREPENTANT   ANTICHRIST'S   EUPHR
JEWS   WORLD   KINGDOM   DRIED
TORMENTED   SCORCHED   TORMENTED   ARMAG
Rev 16:2   BY THE SUN   Rev 16:10-11.   Rev 16
                       Rev 16:8-9.

DOCTRINES
TO INGEST
Rev 16:4-7.

36   37
THE FINAL CALL   THE GATHERING
TO THE WORLD FOR   OF THE WORLD'S
REPENTANCE BEFOR   ARMIES TO ARMAGEDDON
THE OUTPOURING   FOR THE CONCLUSION
OF GOD'S WRATH   OF GOD'S WRATH
Rev 14:6-13.   Rev 14:14-20.

DEATH: TEMPORY ABODE OF DEAD UNFAITHFUL BELIEVERS - NO

HELL: TEMPORY ABODE OF DEAD UNBELIEVERS - CONDEMI

years before the end of two millennia of salvation [c2026AD], which began at the start of Christ's ministr
ation for the salvation of life, two millennia of salvation, and one millennium of rest, which is in accordan
on of life, followed by two days creation of life, and concluded by one day of rest. 2 Pet 3:8. [The prefix

Rev 19:1-18.
CHRIST MARRIES WITH THE
CAUGHT-UP OF THE CHURCHES
THEN DESCENDS WITH THEM
& HIS ANGELS TO EARTH TO
DESTROY THE KINGDOMS OF
MAN & RESTORE THE
KINGDOM OF GOD

Rev 2:16; 3:3;
16:15-16; 19:21.
CHRIST RETURNS
LIKE A THIEF COMES IN
THE NIGHT & SLAYS WITH
THE RIGHTEOUS JUDGMENT
OF HIS WORDS

Rev 2
FIRE FROM
KILLS THE

JP TO ETERNAL LIFE

THFUL BELIEVERS

47

Job 14:12-1

FAITHFUL
REIGN ON EARTH
WITH CHRIST FOR
A MILLENNIUM

Rev 20:7-9
THE NATIONS
OF THE WORLD
GATHER IN
DEFIANCE
OF CHRIST

50

51

44

JERUS

JPHRATES
ED UP FOR
MAGEDDON
v 16 12-16

ALL CITIES OF
MAN, INCLUDING
BABYLON,
FELLED
Rev 16:17-21.

FAITHFUL
JEWS IN
PETRA
SAVED

THE ANTICHRIST
& FALSE PROPHET CAST
INTO THE LAKE OF
FIRE

Rev 19:20

37

BABYLON

46

THE SPIRIT OF
BABYLON
DESTROYED
Rev 18:1-24

SATAN BOUND
DURING
CHRIST'S
REIGN
Rev 20:1-3.

49

NOT YET CONDEMNED

MNED ALREADY   Jn 3:18.

istry [c26AD]. This deduction is based
dance with the pattern established by
efix "C" means approximately]

C2026AD

THE KINGDOM OF GOD RESTORED ON EARTH
FOR A MILLENNIUM WITH CHRIST AS KING

Not to be sold separately. Companion to God's Guide To The End Times. Available

'ULTIMATE DESTINY' KEY

(A) DEAD FAITHFUL OLD TESTAMENT BELIEVERS
(B) DEAD NATIONS JUST KILLED BY FIRE
(C) DEAD UNFAITHFUL BELIEVERS
(D) DEAD UNBELIEVERS
(E) LIVING FAITHFUL BELIEVERS

20:9.
M HEAVEN
E NATIONS

Matt 25:31-34; Jn 5:28-29; Rev 20:11-15.
CHRIST JUDGES THE DEAD

53

Rev 21:1.
HEAVEN
& EARTH
DESTROYED

:1-4.
HEAVE
/ EARTH
EATED

54

SALEM

Rev 20:10.
SATAN CAST
INTO THE
LAKE OF
FIRE

52

THE NEW JERUSALEM
ON THE NEW EARTH:
THE ETERNAL HOME
OF FAITHFUL
BELIEVERS
Rev 21:9-27; 22:1-5.

Lk 12:46; Rev 20:15.
THE LAKE OF FIRE:
THE ETERNAL ABODE
OF THE UNFAITHFUL
& UNBELIEVERS

ETERNITY

C3026AD

THE JUDGING OF THE DEAD, & THE ULTIMATE
DESTINY OF SATAN & ALL HUMANITY

Another book by this Author is *God's Will for Our Daily Lives: The Teaching of Jesus Christ*. Available now from Amazon Books as an E-book, and also soon as an Audio book.

God's Will for Our Daily Lives clearly explains Christ's teaching concerning God's will for daily life. And it shows that His teaching is complete and final.

Other books about God's will for daily life consistently say either that we should, keep the Ten Commandments, live by the New Testament letters, or follow divine inspiration. These are the three main schools of thought today, and they are all flawed.

The Bible clearly says that we are to do what Christ says, and this book clearly explains it. From the basic phases of spiritual growth, to the controversial issue of sin in a believer's life, this book clarifies all of God's will for daily life.

In this ground-breaking explanation of Christ's teaching, you will find God's will clearly defined and explained. You will learn what God requires of every one of us, including:

- Spiritual development - from acceptance of Christ's gospel through to maturity.
- Sacred duty - from enduring persecution to producing a testament.
- Rightness in life - concerning the Mosaic Law, works of faith, and Christ's Law.
- Goodness at heart - in relation to God, possessions, and people.
- Rightness in God's sight - concerning the teaching of man, of Christ, and of the devil.

You will also learn that Christ is the supreme authority concerning God's will, and our complete salvation.

Whether you are a church leader, a Bible believer, or a person yet in search of the Truth, *God's Will For Our Daily Lives* will once and for all resolve any ignorance, misunderstanding, or curiosity, that you may have concerning God's will for your daily life.

Also includes a full colour companion chart, via download or email.

Printed in Poland
by Amazon Fulfillment
Poland Sp. z o.o., Wrocław

371607R00058